THE MAGIC FIGHTS BACK!

EVERYTHING WAS AT PEACE IN THE LUNARY KINGDOM, UNTIL A TERRIBLE CREATURE FROM THE FOREST STARTED TO TERRORIZE THE VILLAGERS IN THE REGION. KNOWING THAT THE PEOPLE WERE FRIGHTENED, KING KRAVUSK SENT THE BRAVE, FEARLESS, AND FAMOUS ARCHER BENNY ALVOR ON A MISSION: TO FIGHT THE MYSTERIOUS CREATURE.

BELIEVING THAT THE TERRIBLE CREATURE WAS MANIPULATED BY MAGIC, BENNY ALVOR WASTED NO TIME AND RUSHED TO THE HOME OF THE WITCH WIKKY, HIS CHILDHOOD FRIEND. THE MOST SKILLFUL ARCHER OF ALL TIME ASKED HER TO CREATE AN ARROW WITH MAGICAL POWERS TO HELP HIM DEFEAT THE CREATURE

THE WITCH WIKKY DID AS BENNY ALVOR ASKED, BUT TOLD HIM TO RETURN THE ARROW AFTER USING IT, FOR THAT POWER COULD NOT FALL INTO THE WRONG HANDS.

LOOKING FOR THE CREATURE, THE ARCHER SOON CAME ACROSS THAT MONSTROUS FIGURE. THEN, HE PREPARED FOR BATTLE AND PLACED HIS MAGIC ARROW INTO THE BOW; HE HAD ONLY ONE CHANCE TO HIT THE CREATURE. LOOKING CLOSELY, THE ARCHER NOTICED THAT THE MONSTER HAD A NECKLACE WITH A POTION AND AIMED HIS ARROW AT THE OBJECT.

WITH NO HESITATION, THE ARCHER BENNY ALVOR AIMED AT THE NECKLACE, SHOT THE MAGIC ARROW, AND HIT THE OBJECT WITH PRECISION, SHATTERING IT INTO PIECES.
TRINK

7

WHEN THE VIAL BROKE, THE STONE CREATURE LOST ITS CHARM, STARTED SHATTERING, AND FELL, CRUMBLING INTO PIECES SPREAD ALL OVER THE FLOOR.

THE RESIDUE FROM THE VIAL, WHICH HAD FALLEN TO THE GROUND, BEGAN TO MOVE IN A STRANGE WAY AND SOON BECAME A DARK SMOKE. IT SUDDENLY CHANGED INTO A FRIGHTENING BEING THAT BEGAN TO SURROUND THE FEARLESS BENNY ALVOR.

WHEN THE SHADOW SAW THE ARROW ON THE GROUND, IT NOTICED THAT THERE WAS SOME KIND OF MAGICAL POWER AROUND IT. THE CREATURE TOOK THE ARROW AND, LOUDLY, SAID:
"I WILL TAKE THIS TO MY MASTER!
HA, HA, HA!"

THE SHADOW HAD THE ARCHER ON THE RUN,
TELLING HIM TO WARN PEOPLE THAT REVERSE
MAGIC WOULD SOON DOMINATE THE KINGDOM.
THUS, THERE WOULD BE ONLY ONE BEING WITH ALL
THE POWER IN THE KINGDOM.

BEFORE RETURNING TO THE KINGDOM, THE ARCHER WENT TO WITCH WIKKY'S HOUSE AND TOLD HER EVERYTHING THAT HAPPENED. BENNY ASKED FOR HELP TO RETRIEVE THE MAGIC ARROW AND SAVE THE KINGDOM FROM THE DOMAINS OF EVIL.

UPON HEARING THE ARCHER'S ACCOUNT, THE WITCH IMMEDIATELY SUSPECTED THAT ALL THIS WAS THE WORK OF MIZYDOR, A SORCERER'S APPRENTICE WHO DISAPPEARED FOR YEARS AFTER STEALING THE BOOK OF MAGIC THAT HAD THE POWER TO CONTROL ELEMENTS OF NATURE. SINCE THEN, ALL POWER HAS BEEN USED FOR EVIL.

13

WIKKY, THE WITCH, PICKED UP HER BROOM
AND DECIDED TO GO ALONE IN SEARCH OF
THE MAGIC ARROW. SHE WAS READY TO FACE
ANY DANGER.

FROM UP ABOVE, THE WITCH WIKKY SPOTTED THE TREE OF KNOWLEDGE AND, APPROACHING IT, WORKED HER MAGIC TO SHOW THE DIRECTION OF THE EVIL SORCERER MIZYDOR. THIS WAY, IT WOULD BE EASY TO FIND IT!

SOON AFTER, WIKKY ARRIVED IN THE MOST DISTANT PART OF THE KINGDOM, WHERE THE BONE SWAMP WAS LOCATED, A FRIGHTENING PLACE THAT WAS HOME TO CREATURES FROM ANOTHER DIMENSION.

AMIDST THE SMOKE, IN A GONDOLA, A MYSTERIOUS BEING APPEARED, WHO SEEMED TO WANT TO PICK HER UP AND TAKE HER SOMEWHERE. WIKKY LOOKED ATTENTIVELY AT THE CREATURE COMING TOWARDS HER.

QUICKLY, THE SORCERER MIZYDOR REVEALED HIMSELF AND RAISED HIS STAFF WITH THE MAGIC ARROW TIED TO IT. THE SHADOW APPEARED TO SERVE THE MAGICIAN, WHO SHOUTED:
"YOU WILL BE MY WITCH, AND YOUR POWER WILL BE MINE!"

THE WITCH PREPARED HER DEFENSE AND THE SORCERER MIZYDOR ATTACKED HER FEROCIOUSLY WITH MYSTICAL BEAMS, TRYING TO HIT HER WITH WICKED ENCHANTMENTS. WIKKY DREW HER MAGIC WAND AND FOUGHT BACK WITH AMAZING SKILL, HITTING THE SHADOW.
VUP
WIK
TUF
SNYK

HOWEVER, AFTER A SLIGHT CARELESSNESS, THE WITCH WAS TRAPPED BY THE THORNY BRANCHES OF THE SWAMP. SHE FOUGHT WITH ALL HER STRENGTH TO GET LOOSE, BUT HER EFFORTS WERE IN VAIN.

WIKKY, THE WITCH, CLOSED HER EYES, CONCENTRATED, AND, AS THE MAGICIAN DIDN'T SHUT HER MOUTH, SHE SUMMONED BEINGS BY CHANTING MAGICAL PHRASES. SOON, SWAMP CREATURES APPEARED TO HELP HER.

21

WIKKY ORDERED THE CREATURES TO TAKE THE MAGIC ARROW BACK, EVEN THOUGH THE MAGICIAN MIZYDOR TRIED TO PLAY SPELLS TO DEFEND HIMSELF. DESPITE EVERYTHING, HE DIDN'T SUCCEED.
22

WITHOUT HIS STAFF AND ARROW OF POWER, THE SORCERER MIZYDOR TRIED TO ESCAPE BY ALL MEANS, BUT HE WAS TRAPPED, AND HIS EVIL PLANS TO DOMINATE THE KINGDOM WERE OVER. NOW, HIS FATE WAS IN WIKKY'S HANDS.

AS A PUNISHMENT, THE WITCH RETRIEVED ALL THE MAGIC BOOKS AND PUT A SPELL ON THE MAGICIAN. IN CASE HE DIDN'T TAKE GOOD CARE OF A SMALL FLOCK OF SHEEP, HE WOULD TURN INTO A PUMPKIN, SO HE WOULDN'T HAVE TIME TO DO EVIL DEEDS.
Vup

THE LITTLE WITCH'S FAME SPREAD THROUGHOUT THE NEIGHBORHOOD. AS SOON AS THE KING LEARNED OF HER BRAVERY AND POWER, HE WAS SO HAPPY WITH THE PROTECTION OF THE KINGDOM THAT HE CALLED WIKKY AND HONORED HER AS THE GOOD WITCH.

FREE FROM EVIL, EVERYONE IN THE KINGDOM WAS HAPPY WHEN THEY SAW WIKKY PASSING BY IN THE SKIES. THE CREATURES OF THE FOREST WERE ALSO JUMPING WITH JOY TO KNOW THAT THEY HAD A GOOD LITTLE WITCH THEY COULD TRUST. THE MAGIC OF LOVE MADE EVERYONE HAPPY FOREVER!